grand master little master
series

sink or
swim

Written by Patricia Merker

Illustrated by Lauren Wilhelm

Foreword

I am pleased to support and boost into form the marvelous content in this Grand Master/ Little Master interactive book series.

I commend talented author Patricia Merker and the sensitive Pick-a-WooWoo publishing team for your combined commitment to bring what I consider universal, peace-making principles into the laps of children and families. This inspired book series combines soul-honoring, character-building, personal-empowerment techniques with balanced mind/body/ spirit activities. The GM/LM series guides children and their families with skillful, playful fun into seeing God as our partner in life. Patricia masterfully brings story into easy living action that articulates in simple and easy-to-live ways how to create a deeply self-inspired AND Divine-inspired lifestyle.

This kind of out-of-the-box educational approach is fundamental to the internationally acclaimed NY Times best selling *Conversations with God (CWG)* series of books and is a mission of the School of the New Spirituality, Inc., the education non-profit founded by author and spiritual leader Neale Donald Walsch.

I'd like to highlight in a concise summary, key principles that the Grand Master/Little Master books bring to life. These foundational beliefs hold inherent power which any parent, grandparent, teacher and all youth professionals may utilize in their work and play with young people to nurture and foster healthy, joyful, loving, honored-for-who-they-are souls:

- God is the All, not any one thing outside of us
- The Divine communicates with us and inside us all the time
- Look for the spark of Source/God, or goodness, in every living being.
- Love is all there is; look inside and see.
- True Love is unconditional, that is it remains without conditions.
- What you CAUSE in the world comes back to you, CAUSE something wonderful today
- Every minute has choice in it. Choose the best for the good of you and for the good of all.
- There is no right or wrong, life is – and we live, learn to love through it all
- Raising children with the belief that they are perfect, magnificent souls on earth will change the world – one healthy child at a time.

As a decade-long co-leader of the School of the New Spirituality, Inc, I professionally endorse Patricia's books. Thank you, Patricia and Pick-a-WooWoo, for this important educational series and contribution to our world.

Linda Lee Ratto EdM, Former Director, Global Education; School of the New Spirituality, Founded by Neale Donald Walsch.

A note from the Author

The Grand Master/Little Master series of books teach, even very young children, about their source of power within. Your child will delight as they follow the journey of the "chosen" little masters in each story. There is no shortage of smiles, admiration and compassion that will warm their hearts and inspire them to re-read these stories over and over.

If however, you choose to take these magical stories to the next level, so begins an interactive adventure in which your child becomes the main character. Minimal parental participation and weekly lessons from Grand Master allow children to address their *own* childhood fears, concerns and self esteem issues.

Universal Laws are presented in ways that give children an opportunity to *experience* their magic rather than to simply read about it. To access the interactive unit of this series which includes how to get started, a synopsis of the lesson associated with each story, a note to the parents, and the weekly lessons from Grand Master to your child, please visit http://www.pickawoowoo.com/childrens-spiritual-books/grand-master-little-master-series/

Enjoy the journey!

Patricia Merker

Patricia can be contacted through her website
http://www.thegrandmasterlittlemasterseries.com/

Summertime! What a perfect time of year! Haley soared through the air on her tire swing. Her dad hung it from the highest branch last summer. She and her little brother, Jordan, thought it was the best swing in the whole world.

School was out and if that wasn't cool enough, there was day camp, bike riding, fireworks, picnics, and parties. There was not *one thing* that she didn't love about summer!

And then she remembered. Suddenly there was a sickening feeling in her stomach. There *was* something that she didn't like about summer. Actually, there was one thing that she *hated* about summer. ***Swimming lessons.*** It was worse than her scariest nightmare!

Her mom and dad insisted that she learn to swim. They said it was important; that she would thank them later, and lots more nonsense that parents go on endlessly about. "Why can't they just leave me alone?" Haley mumbled under her breath. "If I don't care about swimming, why should they?"

At least she had one whole week before her lessons began. Maybe if she pretended hard enough, they would just go away.

Never, *in her entire life*, had one week gone so quickly. The dreaded first morning of swimming lessons arrived in spite of all her pretending. She had to face the water every day for two weeks! *Two lousy weeks!* How can anyone be expected to endure that much pain?

The routine would be the same as before, there was not much point in arguing. She would go to her lesson and cling to the side of the pool until they pried her off. The teacher would take her to the middle of the pool, where she was totally helpless, and expect her to smile while she slowly drowned.

Every day last summer she did the same thing and her parents continued to make her take lessons. "I'll never learn to swim, I hate it," she said out loud. "Why won't anyone listen to me? I can't do it!"

She had been in the same class for three years; they never passed her. It was totally embarrassing. All the kids in her class were four and five years old. Haley was eight. She felt like the queen nerd. Maybe their plan was to shame her into learning to swim. After looking at the kids in her class this year, *it just might work.*

One of the lifeguards blew an obnoxious whistle.

"All level one students, in the water please!" she shouted. All the little kids either jumped in the water, or walked down the ladder Haley could tell they weren't afraid. At least, not like she was.

What's wrong with me? She thought.

"Are you in *this* class?" asked a little boy who was hanging on to the ladder.

"Yeah, what of it?" Haley asked, glaring at him rudely.

"You're so big!" he giggled. "You look totally freaked out! Are you afraid?"

"Yeah, I guess I am," she replied, realizing that the look of terror on her face was a dead give-away.

"Are *you* afraid?" she asked.

"Nah, not of water. But I'm *really* scared of the dark. Are you afraid of the dark?" he asked.

"Not really" she answered, without even hearing what he said. Haley felt her hands begin to tremble. It was so weird how her entire body felt scared. Her parents kept saying that it was all in her head, but she knew better. It felt like it was in every part of her body and she couldn't control it.

I can't do this, I really can't, she panicked.

The little boy put his head under the water and paddled off.

"Come on in to me," said the lifeguard, seeing that Haley was terrified. She extended her arms to help her in the water. "Don't be frightened, I've got you," she said.

But Haley *was* frightened. The other children seemed to be having fun. They were laughing and playing. Maybe she just wasn't trying hard enough. She'd have to try harder! Maybe she could do it after all, just like her mom and dad told her.

The lifeguard asked her to float on her back on top of the water. "I won't let you sink, trust me. Just lay back on my hands."

It was no use. Her whole body was trembling and it felt as heavy as concrete. She was so terrified that she couldn't breathe! Every time something inside of her said, *"you can do this,"* something else louder screamed, ***"no you can't***! Her body collapsed at the waist. *Not* a great position for floating. She begged the lifeguard to take her back to the side of the pool. Haley realized that she was even more afraid than last year, if that was possible. She felt like a total failure.

When the grueling half-hour had ended, Haley saw the instructor talking with her mom. It didn't look good. She knew it was going to be a long ride home.

They drove for at least five minutes in total silence. Finally, her mom said, "What are we going to do, Haley?"

"I don't know, mom, I can't do it," Haley said with tears streaming down her face. "I want to, but I just can't."

Her mom softened. "I'm sorry you're so scared, sweetie. Let's give it one or two more days and if it doesn't get better, we'll stop. Maybe when you get older you'll outgrow some of the fear. How does that sound?"

"Okay," Haley said, as she wiped her eyes.

That should have made her feel happy, but for some reason she felt very sad and lonely.

When Haley woke up the next morning, she felt something under her pillow. It was a letter from Grand Master! She was filled with a warm, wonderful feeling. Grand Master always understood her. The letter read:

Dear Little Master,

When someone does something brave, it is not because they are not afraid! Everyone has fear at some time in his or her life, Little Master. The choice is whether you have it, or it has you. Choose one, because it truly is a choice." Let me explain:

If the fear has you, you think it is real. The voice of fear is telling you that you cannot swim, and you believe it! What you believe becomes so. It will live in every cell of your body. *That voice is not who you are.*

If, however, you choose to have the fear, you will know that by ignoring it, you will silence it. It cannot survive without your attention. It would serve you well to listen instead, to the soft, gentle voice that says; "I am able; I am wonderful; I am pure spirit." That is Truth. It is the voice of your soul. *It is I, Little Master.*

How do you know that I speak the Truth? Ask your heart. It feels right, doesn't it, Little Master? That voice too, will get louder the more you listen, and you will listen and begin to trust it because the Truth will bring you much joy. Always check your heart. You will find your answers there.

Whatever you choose is up to you. It is okay to choose either. But be very clear that the choice is yours and **you can change your listening whenever you want**. The voice of your soul knows what you are capable of; the other voice does not. **Which voice will you listen to tomorrow?** I am always with you.

I love you,
Grand Master

The sun beamed brightly in Haley's window the next morning. It seemed to say, "Rise and shine, it's a beautiful day!" She didn't know why but she felt good today. *Is this day different somehow*, she thought, *or am I different?*

If what Grand Master said was true, and it always was, then she really could swim if she chose to. *She* was the only thing getting in her way! It was a silly but exciting thought!

The butterflies in her stomach were still there, but there was something else there too. It was a voice, a soft voice, or maybe a feeling, she wasn't sure. But clearly it was a good thing. She thought that she might choose to swim today.

As the car neared the pool, that scary feeling started to return. The usual doubt and fear sat in her belly like a bowling ball. *"I can't do this,"* she started to think. And then she remembered what Grand Master had said:

"If the fear has **you**, Little Master, you think it is real. The voice of fear is telling you that you cannot swim, and you believe it! What you believe becomes so. It will live in every cell of your body. That voice is not who you are."

Its not who I am and it's definitely not who I want to be! she thought.

"Mom, I'm going to swim today", Haley said with an air of confidence that her mother had not recently heard.

"No kidding?" asked her mom.

"No kidding," said Haley. I'm still scared but I'm just going to ignore my fear today. I'm tired of letting it tell me what I can or can't do!"

"That's great honey. What's with the sudden confidence?"

"Well, a good friend told me that fear is just something I can *have*. I don't have to pay any attention to it if I don't want to. I really don't want to mom. I want to swim. It looks like fun!"

"It is sweetie and you are such an enlightened little girl," responded her mom. "Do you know that most adults go through their entire lives and never know that little secret? They think the fear is real and it runs their life. Your friend must be very smart."

"Oh, she is," said Haley smiling.

Haley sat by the side of the pool, dangling her legs in the water, waiting for the whistle to blow.

She had the feeling that something was *missing*. Could it be the nagging voice of fear? Strange, she hadn't even noticed it being there before, like a voice, until Grand Master pointed it out. How could something so loud go unnoticed? She didn't think that she would ever *not notice* that voice again if it came back, and she thought that it might.

The water was *sort of* nice this morning. Sometimes it felt like ice, or, maybe it was her body that sometimes felt frozen, she wasn't sure.

The whistle blew and Haley's heart skipped a beat. "All level one students in the water please!" yelled the instructor.

She confidently walked over to the ladder. She backed down the rungs until the water reached her neck. She suddenly felt like she couldn't breathe.

"*You can't do this,*" said the fear, and her body began to shake.

"I *can* do this" replied Haley. "*Watch me.*"

"Okay," said her instructor, assuming she was talking to her. "You'll be okay, Haley. Take my hands and try to relax."

"*I can do this, I can do this,*" she kept saying over and over, and for the first time ever, she believed it.

And she did. Haley had her very first real swimming lesson. She chose to listen, for the first time, to the instructor, instead of the fear. It wasn't that the voice went completely away; it was just that it had no audience!

She felt awesome! The water felt awesome! Life is good, she thought.

"So, how do you feel?" asked her mom on their way home from a very successful swimming lesson.

"I feel happy, I feel proud, I feel able, wonderful and magnificent!" Haley practically shouted, meaning every word of it.

"You know mom, I felt like I was in jail or something. The fear was so real. It still sorta is, but I know that it's always my choice, and that feels better. It's like I can change things anytime I want, or not!"

"Yes ma'am, and almost everything in life is like that," replied her mother.

"But mom, some fear is good, right? I mean, if a stranger asked me to get into his car, *that* would be scary. But I shouldn't do it. Or if someone tried to get me to do drugs at school, that would be scary. I know you wouldn't want me to do that!"

"Yes honey, that's right. Whenever you are in doubt, just see how your heart feels about it. Your heart always knows. For example, didn't you know, *in your heart,* that your fear of swimming was unnecessary? Don't you also know that drugs and scary strangers should be avoided because they are dangerous?"

"Yeah, I guess I do. Just ask my heart, huh? It always knows?" Funny, Grand Master told her the same thing.

"It always knows," responded her mother. "Sometimes we don't *want* to hear the answer, but it always knows. Sometimes we will choose to *ignore* it, but we still know. We'll talk about this anytime that you have questions – if you want. I'd be honored if you would share your tough questions with me! I may not always have the answers, but I'll do my best to help you find what is right for *you*."

"Thanks mom, I have another good friend that does the same thing for me. She's very special and very wise."

"I'd very much like to meet her sometime," said her mom.

"Oh, I feel certain that you will," smiled Haley.

The last day of swimming lessons had finally arrived. Haley knew that she would pass this year. She also decided to take level two, right away, after level one was over. Maybe by next summer she could catch up to the other kids her age!

She was feeling like quite the little otter. Although she hadn't mastered swimming across the pool yet, she certainly had learned a few things. She learned that if she held her breath and went all the way under, it felt very much like playing in a big bowl of Jell-O! She learned that floating was quite natural and easy when her body wasn't desperately fighting it. And, she learned that if she would quit laughing so hard, she wouldn't swallow so much water! Her instructor told her she would be swimming in the deep end in just a few days if she kept practicing.

She was thinking a lot about Grand Master this morning. As a 'Little Master in training,' Haley knew that she would be expected to help others along the way. She learned that we are all part of a big 'Oneness' of the Universe. Grand Master told her once that it is the reason we are all here, to help others. By helping others, she was doing something wonderful that came back to her!

She imagined all the other things that kids could be afraid of. The little boy at the pool is afraid of the dark, she thought. One of her friends from school is terrified of height. The fears *seem* different, but it's really all the same. I guess fear is fear!

Before her last lesson began that morning, she caught a glimpse of the little boy that spoke to her on the first day of lessons. "Hello!" she shouted, waving her arms to get his attention. The little boy looked up and Haley motioned him to come over. He dove under the water and swam to her.

"What's your name?" she asked. "I don't think you ever told me."

"Timmy," the boy responded. "What's yours?"

"I'm Haley. It's so nice to meet you!"

"You don't look afraid of the water anymore," Timmy said.

"Nope, I'm not. Turns out it was all in my head, but man, it was a nightmare that lasted for three summers!"

"So, what happened?" asked Timmy.

"I have a very good friend that helps me when I need it."

"Maybe I could talk to your friend cause I'm still afraid of the dark. I know that I make it all up but it still ruins my nights. It's real bad and I wake my parents up a lot."

"Sounds like the fear has *you*, instead of you having *it,* doesn't it?"

Timmy looked at her like she was from another planet. "I'm not sure exactly what you mean but it sounds right," Timmy answered.

"I've got something to share with you that will change your life,

21

Tim, no kidding." Haley said as though she were a Little Master already. "After class I'll tell you all about it, okay?"

"You bet!" Timmy said excitedly, and off he swam.

"Strange," Haley thought, "Grand Master taught me that what I put out in the world comes back to me. She said it was one of the great Universal Principles; *what goes around, comes around.* And it was true, she thought. By helping Timmy and making *him* feel good, she got to feel good too!

"This is good stuff!" she said out loud, and as she jumped into the water she had the feeling that all was right in the world. She felt whole, complete and magnificent! She knew that there was nothing she couldn't do.

Pick-a-Woo Woo

National Library of Australia Cataloguing-in-Publication entry
Author –Merker, Patricia,
Title: Sink or swim / by Patricia Merker; Illustrated by Lauren Wilhelm
Edition: 1st ed.
ISBN 9780980652079 (pbk.)
Series: Merker, Patricia. Grand master, little master; bk. 2
Other Contributors: Wilhelm, Lauren
Dewey Number A8234

Publishing Details
Published in Australia - Pick-A-Woo Woo Publishers
www.pickawoowoo.com

Printed
Lightning Source (US/UK/EUR/AUS)

Channels / Distribution

United States
Ingram Book Company; Amazon.com; Baker & Taylor

Canada
Chapters Indigo; Amazon Canada

United Kingdom
Amazon.com; Bertrams; Book Depository Ltd; Gardners; Mallory International

Australia

DA Information Services; The Nile; Emporium Books Online; James Bennet (Australian Libraries)
Dennis Jones and Associates; Brumby Books and Music

Other Books in the Grand Master Little Master Series

Book One
The Karate Tournament
Meet Grand Master
Topic: Cause and Effect

Grand Master says:
"What you *CAUSE* in the world comes back to you
Little Master. *CAUSE* something wonderful today!"

The Karate Tournament is the first book and the foundation for all subsequent books in *The Grand Master/Little Master series*. This book is your child's introduction to Grand Master and his/her invitation to go on a life-changing adventure!

When eight-year-old Haley's mother asks her if she would like to play a game on the morning of her karate tournament, she is somewhat reluctant, given all the butterflies in her stomach! Not quite able to resist the temptation, however, she agrees. Grand Master (who makes His/Her presence known through mom in this first story) tells Haley that she has been chosen to be a Little Master-in-training and there is much to do. What follows is a heart warming story of a little girl who learns the importance and magic of Cause and Effect; what goes around, comes around. "What you put out in the world comes back, Little Master; cause love, cause kindness, cause forgiveness. Try not to cause sadness or anger. This too, must come back." This is the story of Haley, and how she turns a very scary and nervous situation into a joyous occasion by her conscious use of Law.

Book Three
Love has many faces.
Topic: Love (in all its forms!)

Grand Master says:
"Love is all there is, Little Master. Sometimes it does not look like love, but it is.
I am *love,* I am *you,*
I am the world and I live inside the soul of every living being. See if you can find me where you think I am not!"

Love Has Many Faces is the third book in *The Grand Master/Little Master series* and addresses the" less than loving" people in our life.

Jordan is anxious to start first grade and can't wait to meet his new teacher! You can imagine his dismay when he realizes that he is to spend an entire school year with a crotchety teacher that is not very nice to the class, and especially seems to not like *him*. Read this heart-warming story of a young boy who follows Grand Master's advice, and looks deeper than the surface to find an expression of love.

9 780980 652079